A strange vision
on Aarslev meadows
in the year 1600

As documented by
Holger Rosenkrantz

A strange vision
on Aarslev meadows
in the year 1600

As documented by
Holger Rosenkrantz

With commentary
by
Jesper M. Paasch

Veidarvon

© 2015 Jesper Mayntz Paasch
ISBN 978-91-982058-0-0

Publisher:
Veidarvon, Sweden
www.veidarvon.com
veidarvon@telia.com

Print: www.lulu.com

Disclaimer:
The text published here has been translated to the best of my
ability and no responsibility can be taken regarding the
correctness of the translation, the vision itself, the
interpretation of it or the names of persons.

Table of Content

1 Introduction

This publication is, to the best of my knowledge, the first English translation of an account describing a strange vision near the small village of Aarslev on the Jutland peninsula in Denmark on April 30th in the year 1600. Aarslev is located south of the city of Randers on the Jutland peninsula. Aarslev is spelled "Årslev" in modern Danish. See the map in section 2.

The vision has been subject to much speculation about what the witnesses observed; being an omen and sign of God, a strange weather phenomenon or more spectacular interpretations such as an extraterrestrial visit and UFO landing. The event is in Danish popular literature sometimes called the first Danish UFO sighting.

I do not in any way present an explanation concerning the nature of the vision and do not put forth any interpretation myself. This publication does not claim to be more than an attempt to present this interesting event to an English speaking audience.

Details of the vision are delivered to us by the Danish nobleman and scholar Holger Rosenkrantz. He documented the event by interviewing the eyewitnesses shortly after the vision occurred.

Rosenkrantz's original Danish language document is believed to have been lost when a fire occurred in the Rosenkrantz family archives in the 19th century. However, the account has luckily survived to this day due to being copied by the historian Jacob Langebek in around 1760. The first two pages of his copy are shown below. The handwritten document is now in the Danish Royal Library, Copenhagen. Langebek´s copy has served as source for printed versions by H. F. Rørdam in 1886 and S. Hansen in 1909.

The text published here is kept close to the original wording, except that a more modern grammar is applied for the benefit of contemporary readers. Lengthy, religious passages praising God, frequently used in 16th-17th century texts, have been shortened. I use the term "peasant" in the summary and explanatory notes as a general synonym for the eyewitnesses, being persons of inferior social standing and usually engaged in agricultural labour.

Chapter 2 contains an overview of the topography of Aarslev Meadows. Chapter 3 provide an introduction to Holger Rosenkrantz. A summary of Rosenkrantz´s account can be found in chapter 4. The translation of the account in chapter 5 follows Langebek´s copy with minor additional explanations placed in brackets [ ]. Chapter 6 contains a list of names of people who had the vision. The list seems not to have been published until now. Explanatory notes concerning details in the translated text can be found in chapter 7. References are placed in chapter 8.

The reason for Rosenkrantz´s interest in the vision is unknown, but an explanation may be that the event was seen as an act of God, which he mentions in the beginning of the account. He was a devoted Christian as well as having a scholarly and theological interest, which may explain why he wanted to investigate the strange event.

Rosenkrantz did for unknown reasons not seem to have published the story. Research in Danish archives has not produced any results, as mentioned by Hansen in connection with his 1909 publication of the account. My own research in Danish archives has also been fruitless in obtaining older documents than Langebek´s copy.

I would like to thank everyone who has shown an interest in this little book, especially Anna Forsberg, for input, support and always constructive criticism; Kasper M. Paasch for valuable advice; and Hamish Brett and Dr. John Nandris for valuable advice on language issues.

I hope the book will act as input for further research and discussions of what happened on the last day of April outside a small village in Denmark 415 years ago.

Jesper Mayntz Paasch

April 2015

En Pandru og udførlig Beretning
Om det

... som Gud allermægtigste ... kaldt ... i Judtland, den første
Aprilis ... først forladt 1600. ...
... flid efter alle Omstændigheder indspurt
og antegnet

Herrens Rige Rommer.

Job. XII.

Det er lovligt at aabenbare Herrens gjerninger.

Psal. XCII.

Herre hvor ere dine Gjerninger store?
og dine tanker saa meget dybe. Et gal
Menneske troer det ikke, og en gal
agter ikke saadant.

Title page of Langebek's 18th century copy of Rosenkrantz's account. © The Royal Library, Copenhagen

Der ligger en liden landsbye i Judtland
en stor half miil i Sudost fra Randers
strax ved Brabjerig ... Niels Krabbes
Gaard Bruusgaard, ved Navn Barslos. der
... ...
... Aprilis ...
... ...
... ...
... ...
... og ... ...
forsamled, sagde ... af bønderne, som var
Oldermand der i byen, ved Navn Niels Mikkelsen, ... Jørgen ... ... Skaane,
at oftbe?. Møllerne i Bruusgaards Mølle,
som ligger der ... ... fand nu maaled,
og de ... derfor ... meget ... i Aar,
da kunde de der intet udrette, og ...

Page from Langebek's 18th century copy of Rosenkrantz account. © The Royal Library, Copenhagen

2 Aarslev Meadows

Aarslev Meadows are located southwest of the small village of Aarslev, approx 10 kilometres / 6.2 miles south of the city of Randers on the Jutland peninsula in Denmark.

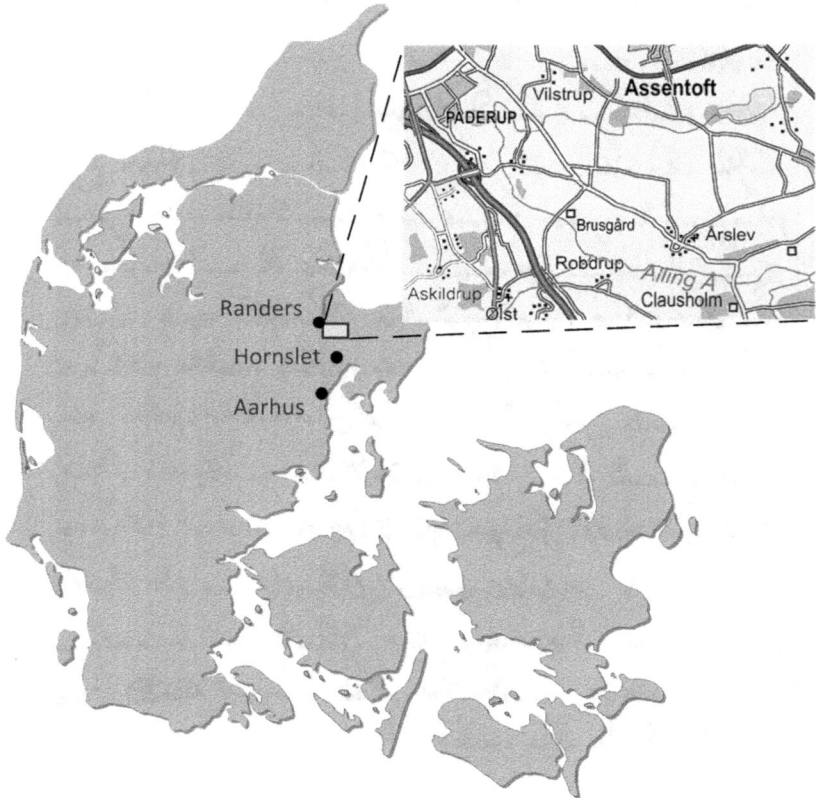

Map of the Jutland peninsula, Denmark. The insert map show the location of Aarslev [Årslev], Brusgaard [Brusgård] and Robdrup, mentioned in Rosenkrantz's account. © Based on MapResources.com, and Danish Geodata Agency (DTK/kort200, January 2015)

The landscape around Aarslev has only undergone few changes during the last four centuries due to farming and drainage of wetlands. The meadows are not as prominent as in Rosenkrantz's days, but are still recognizable in the landscape today. The stream, Alling Å, running through the meadows in 1600, still exists, together with other topographical features mentioned in his account. The forest shown to the upper left in the map below is most likely "Brusgaard Forest" mentioned in his account. The extension of the forest may of course have changed during the centuries.

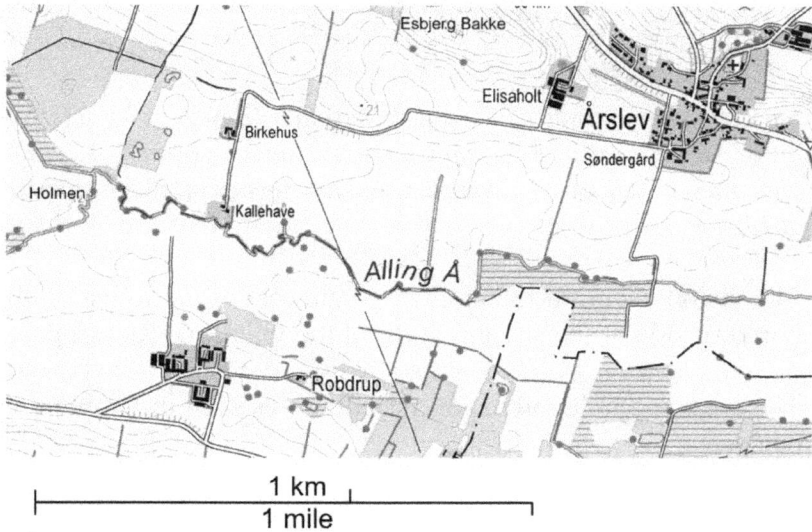

20th century map showing Aarslev village, the stream (Alling Å) south of Aarslev, Robdrup and Brusgaard Forest in the upper left corner. © Danish Geodata Agency. (K25T, January 2015)

It is possible to get an impression of the extent of the wetlands in 1600 by studying a late 19th century map of the area where they are more dominant than today.

Late 19th century map of Denmark showing "Brusgaard Forest" in the upper left corner, Robdrup village, the meadows south of Aarslev and Aarslev village. © Danish Geodata Agency. (M20H, January 2015)

The vision occurred rather close to the east of the forest on the northern side of the stream, north of the village of Robdrup.

The areas are today used for agriculture as seen in the pictures below.

Photo of Aarslev Meadows taken from Robdrup facing north.
© *Author*

Photo of Aarslev Meadows taken from northeast, towards Robdrup.
© *Author*

3 Holger Rosenkrantz

Holger Rosenkrantz was born in 1574. He spent much of his life at Rosenholm Castle, which he inherited from his father. Rosenholm is located a few kilometres outside the village of Hornslet, approx. 25 km / 15.5 miles southeast of Randers.

Rosenholm Castle. © Author

The Rosenkrantz family was one of the most influential noble families in Denmark during the 16th and 17th centuries. Holger Rosenkrantz is probably the most well known member of the family. He was called "the Learned" by his contemporaries due to his intellectual interests. He studied theology, languages and law abroad in his youth, e.g. at the university in Wittenberg in Germany. Mainly theology caught his interest and he corresponded during his lifetime with theological scholars and others in Europe, e.g. the famous Danish astronomer Tycho Brahe, living in Prague in present day Czech republic.

Rosenkrantz held several high positions in society and was on several occasions representing King Kristian IV of Denmark in matters of state. In 1616, the king requested Rosenkrantz to join the Privy Council. The Council consisted of counsellors to the king and was hugely influential in matters of State. The counsellors were chosen from the society's elite. He accepted the nomination and became the sixth generation of the family to serve as counsellor. In 1627 he however decided to resign from the Council, which was an act unheard of. A seat in the Council was expected to be for life and the decision made the king disappointed and angry.

Contributing to the king's strong reaction was that Rosenkrantz made his decision in a time when Denmark was in great danger. Europe was being ravaged by the 30-year war (1618-1648) and enemy forces were invading parts of Denmark. However, he wanted to devote his time to religious studies instead of politics.

The painting below shows Rosenkrantz at the age of 33. He is dressed as a young nobleman in a costly embroidered costume and armed with a high quality rapier sword and dagger, all indicating his high status in society. The painting has Danish text that translates as "Holger Rosenkrantz the Learned from Rosenholm", "Anno CHRI: 1607". His right hand, holding a rose, rests on a book, possibly a bible. The Latin phrase "Memento Mori" [i.e. "Remember that You must Die"] is written on the edge of the table.

Holger Rosenkrantz the Learned. Painted in 1607. © The Museum of National History, Frederiksborg Castle, Denmark

Rosenkrantz published during his lifetime several works on theological subjects and was critical of the orthodox interpretation of the Lutheran Christian philosophy practiced in his days. His views were new and not easily accepted among the orthodox Danish clergy.

He also had a strong interest in education and founded a private school at Rosenholm. Family and friends sent their children in great numbers to be educated.

Rosenkrantz even took part in local community affairs and e.g. founded a library and a hospital in the nearby Hornslet village.

He was married to Sophie Brahe, by whom he had 13 children. 8 children reached adulthood and 3 sons held high official positions during their lifetimes. Holger Rosenkrantz died in 1642.

As a peculiar note, someone familiar with Shakespeare's famous play "Hamlet" may recognise the Rosenkrantz name as belonging to one of two companions in the play; Rosencrantz and Guildenstern. It is known that a member of the Rosenkrantz family, Frederik Rosenkrantz, visited the royal English court in 1592 together with another Danish noble, Knud Gyldenstjerne. They are regarded as possible sources for the names in the play.

4 Summary of Rosenkrantz's account from 1600

On April 30th in 1600 a group of peasants met on the meadows southwest of small village of Aarslev. They had planned to clean the local stream running through the meadows. They could however not perform their task due to high water level.

While resting on the ground before departing home one of them, Niels Mikkelsen, saw what to him seemed to be a large carriage and a group of persons coming down the meadow near Brusgaard Forest approx. 600 meters / 656 yards away, and towards the peasants. The strangers were running around amongst themselves in a disorderly manner and slowly moving towards them.

The others did at first not believe him and said it must be cattle coming down the meadow since no nobleman's carriage could access the wet area. However, when looking themselves they also saw the carriage and the strangers running around among each other as they came closer towards them.

The strange crowd consisted of tall and corpulent persons much higher than people normally are. All seemed to be dressed in black, except two tall, but thin persons who were dressed in red, and a third person dressed in a long white garment reaching down to his feet.

The white person seemed to remain on the south side of the group or was amongst the others a few times, depending on the individual eyewitness accounts. The two red persons were running rapidly in and out of the crowd. It seemed that they were all running around amongst each other as if they were playing or fighting. They had long staves with very shiny iron ends, with which they used to sting each other and sometimes used to lift each other into the air. Especially the two red strangers seemed to have much to do among the others. It seemed the peasants that a kind of smoke was hanging over the strangers when they were together. The smoke disappeared when they moved away from each other, but returned when they came closer again.

It seemed when the strangers had come a little closer that one of them had a huge long shiny iron with which he cut among the others, like a broadsword. The peasants and the women accompanying them were very frightened and prayed to God that the strangers would move away from, not towards, them.

They noticed, after having watched the spectacle for about 30 minutes, two persons who seemed to be other peasants coming from the nearby village of Robdrup south of the vision. The two were walking on the other side of the strange crowd, much closer to them than as they were. However, inquiries in the village the next day were negative since no one claimed to have been in that area or had seen anything.

At about the same time as they saw the two peasants, one of the strangers ran out of the crowd. It seemed that he was wearing a large white object like a hat on his head. He ran with great force towards the earlier mentioned tall person wearing the white garment standing south of the strange crowd. The white person then ran up the meadow being chased by the other. It then seemed the peasants that the white went into the crowd and all then seemed to run hastily westwards up the meadow towards Brusgaard Forest where they came from.

The peasants observed the black strangers disappearing before their eyes, whereas they clearly could see the red strangers in front of, behind, among and sometimes on all sides of the crowd before they all vanished into the air.

On their way home the peasants met some boys who were herding pigs and asked them if they had witnessed anything. They said no, but said they have heard so heavy a rain shower and storm that it frightened them. It seemed that the trees were shaking when it came over the forest.

News of the vision spread in the local community. It was announced in churches and at the local district court, which also functioned as a place for spreading news of interest to the local community. Holger Rosenkrantz heard about the vision and wanted to investigate it.

Rosenkrantz travelled in the morning of the 2nd day of Pentecost (May 12th) to Aarslev Church, where he let the local priest, Mr. Hans Pedersen, summon to him and spoke with him about the event. The priest told the same story he later heard from the eyewitnesses, but not with the same amount of detail. In addition to this, the priest also mentioned that he himself on the day of the vision had been in a nearby forest to attend to his cattle, which were grazing in the forest and attended by a shepherd boy. On his way home he heard the sound of bad weather and thunder above his head. At the same time a voice clearly and unquestionably shouted WÆ, WÆ, WÆ, which frightened him a lot and left him standing paralysed in the forest for a moment. The priest went back to the boy to ask if he had heard anything, too. He had not, except from the sound of a heavy rain shower and storm wind. On his way back to the village the priest met the Aarslev peasants, who told him about their frightening experience.

Rosenkrantz thereafter spoke with several of the people present in the churchyard and asked them to stay until after the service. He then interviewed 15 or 16 of them individually at the church altar. After having conducted the interviews he asked them to come to his residence, probably Rosenholm Castle, to tell their stories to his servants and others. Four peasants came to Rosenholm the same afternoon and retold their stories to Rosenkrantz´s servants and others, being an audience of more than 50 persons.

5 Rosenkrantz´s account from 1600

A true and detailed account concerning the strange vision that God the Almighty did let happen in Jutland on the last day of April in 1600. Researched and documented with considerable effort.

The Realm of the Lord is coming

Tob. XII

It is allowed to show the Deeds of the Lord.

Psal. XCII

Lord, Your Deeds are great and Your Thoughts are deep!

An insane Person does not believe it

And a Jester does not notice it.

There is a small village called Aarslev in Jutland a large half mile southeast of Randers, next to nobleman Niels Krabbes farm Brusgaard. Common townsmen had in this year 1600 agreed to meet on the last day of April [April 30th] on the meadows south of the village to clean the stream, which run trough it.

When most of them had arrived about between 10 and 11 before noon, one of the men, Niels Mikkelsen, who was aldermand of the village [i.e. a leading person in the local community], *and a servant* [see note 1] *of Jørgen Bille in Skåne, said there was too much water in the stream because Brusgaard Mølle* [i.e. Brusgaard Mill, the local water powered mill], *was grinding* [i.e. resulting in a high water level]. *He said they might as well go home and meet another day to continue the work. At the same time he looked away from the group, which consisted of about 15 or 16 persons resting on the meadows. One group was on one side of the stream and one group on the other side.*

When Niels Mikkelsen stood and looked in the direction of Brusgaard Forest to the west, he thought that far away across the meadows there emerged a large carriage with people and many others running around and rapidly coming down on the meadow. He therefore called upon the others resting on the meadow that they should get up and watch, since it seemed to him that something was coming down the meadow towards them. They however thought he was joking and wanted to frighten them.

One of the men, Peder Tordsen, His Royal Majesty's servant at Dronningborg [see note 2] *got up from the ground and came to the aforementioned Niels Mikkelsen. He showed him where they were approaching, to which he answered that it must be cattle running around since no nobleman's carriage could access this large marsh. It seemed to be three musket-shots* [approx. 600 metres / 650 yards, see note 3] *away from them.*

At last it seemed that they [the strangers] *parted from each other and came closer. They* [the peasants] *then shouted to each other and came closer together. The aforementioned Peder Tordsen said: "Eja! It is true! I think they are fighting!"*

They all saw a crowd of tall and corpulent persons, much higher above their shoulders than people normally are. All seemed to be [dressed in?] *black apart from two tall, but thin, persons who were* [dressed in?] *red like blood and another dressed in a long white garment reaching down to the feet.*

The aforementioned Peder Tordsen especially told that he with great care had watched the person in white and thought he had a black band [belt?] *round him and that the white garment was split up to the knee on one side. They all said that the white person stayed much on the south side of the group and stood still. Only the aforementioned Niels Mikkelsen claimed that this white* [person] *also was amongst the others a few times.*

They all said they watched the two red persons running fast in and out of the crowd; one to the south and the other to the north and then back towards each other into the crowd again. When they came back to the crowd they [all] *ran amongst each other, back and forth, to all sides and around as if they were playing or fighting. They had long staves with very shiny iron on the top, with which they used to sting each other and sometimes used to lift each other up into the air. It especially looked like the two red ones had much to do among the others. It seemed that a kind of smoke was over them when they were together. Sometimes they moved away from each other and then there was no smoke, but the smoke reappeared over them as soon as they moved towards each other again.*

When they [the strangers] *had come very close, they shouted to one of their fellow townsmen by the name of Staphen Pedersen, a middle-aged man who was ploughing nearby, that he should come to them and watch what was happening. He said that he also witnessed it all when he came. He and the others mentioned the great fear and terror expressed by the poor women who also were present around him, shouting and screaming that he should help them. They all mentioned that he told Niels Mikkelsen (who also admitted that he was very afraid): 'Let us turn to God and pray that this will turn away from us and not towards us.' Around that time they saw the strangers interact with* [and come closer towards?] *each other near their* [the peasants] *field beside the meadow. Some said that they could see that one had a huge long shiny and glimmering iron* [staff?]*, like a broadsword, which he used to cut among the others.*

When the activities had lasted for more than half an hour they all said they saw two men coming from a village named Ruptrup [spelled Robdrup today] *located straight opposite* [of the strange crowd?]*. The men were walking through a small thicket, which they called Ruptrup Kjær and went down on the other side of the* [strange] *crowd. The aforementioned Aarslev people said they therefore later would ask them, who they thought to be Ruptrup men, about the incident since they had been much closer to the vision than themselves. When they asked in the village the next day, nobody had been down there or knew anything about it.*

They also said that at the same time as those two came walking, one [stranger] *which seemed to have a tall, white thing on his head like a hat ran out of the crowd and with great power came towards the aforementioned one standing south* [of the strange crowd]*, wearing this long white garment.*

27

It then seemed that he [the white stranger] *suddenly ran away up the meadow. The people saw this and said to each other: "Did you see how this person chased away the white?" At the same time they all* [the crowd] *also ran with great speed westwards up the meadow, where they came from.*

There are some fields extending onto the meadow. They are called Birkehovedet [in English: the Birchhead]; *It seemed them that it* [it is unclear what "it" means] *came over, and that at about the same time the white one went into the crowd to the others and suddenly moved sideward with others towards nobleman Niels Krabbes Forest* [Brusgaard Forest] *where they at last disappeared before their eyes.*

During the time they [the strangers] *moved away from them* [the peasants] *the blacks faded more and more before their eyes, whereas they clearly could see the reds in front of, behind, sometimes among and on all sides until they all vanished before their eyes. One of the men, the aforementioned Niels Mikkelsen, ran after them over 20 or 30 acres* [see note 4]. *He asked the others to join him, but they were afraid and stayed behind until the vision disappeared before their eyes.*

They all told how they often asked each other whether they had observed the same, asking: "I observed it this way, did you also observe it that way?", etc. So many strange things had happened that it was impossible for them to remember or tell all that had happened before their eyes.

I have investigated and documented everything described here with the greatest care, so that all God obedient people shall know that it is not composed of some loose tidings or the talk of careless people and gossip.

I drove in the morning on the second day of Pentecost [i.e. May 12th 1600] *to Aarslev Church after having heard about it* [the vision] *in numerous places and in different versions and even had noticed that it had been announced by their parish priest in both churches and in their local district court, Hald Herredsting* [see note 5]. *I was accompanied by the well educated master Niels Paaske* [see note 6].

Aarslev Church. © *Author*

When I arrived in good time at the church, which is located in the village, I let the local priest, by the name of Mr. Hans Pedersen, a good and honest Danish citizen, summon to me on the churchyard. I spoke with him alone and asked if he had heard anything [about the vision] **and instructed him to tell me what his parish members had told him.**

He then told me approximately the same as I have documented here, but not as detailed as I later heard from the townsmen myself, having most eagerly asked them. This shall be communicated later [in this document].

In addition to all this he told me that on the same day [of the vision] *he went to the forest not far from where the townsmen later told that the vision vanished before their eyes. When he came into the forest he heard the clock at Brusgaard strike eleven. He then went a little further into the forest to attend to his cattle. His cattle had suffered from the strong winter and he told his shepherd boy to guard them carefully and lead them to the scarce grass growing that time of the year.*

The priest said that when he was on his way home after having attended to his cattle about half an hour and about one or two stone throws away from the boy he heard a terrible sound of bad weather and thunder above his head and a voice which clearly and unquestionable shouted WÆ, WÆ, WÆ. This frightened him a lot and left him standing paralysed on the spot for a moment. After a while he went back to the boy and asked if he had heard any shouting in forest. The boy said he heard the sound of a heavy rain shower and storm wind. He then asked if he had heard anything else, to which the boy answered no.

Then the aforementioned Mr. Hans Pedersen left the forest heading towards the village and met the earlier mentioned people who have witnessed the earlier mentioned vision [see note 7]. *They told him with great fear and horror what they had seen below the meadow, which he understood had occurred at the same time as he heard the shouting. He stated by the mercy of God that it was true. He gave me his written account later and he stated before God the Almighty and all people that it is a true account. I have his account for safekeeping.*

After hearing this from him I spoke with many of the townspeople present at the churchyard and asked those who had witnessed it to stay after church service since I would like to hear from them what truly happened. I spoke with them again after the service and there came as many of them as were attending the service, which was 15 or 16 persons, both men and women.

The seven oldest and most esteemed persons were Niels Mikkelsen, Jørgen Bildes servant; Staphen Pedersen, Eske Brokkes servant [see note 8]; Peder Tordsen, His Royal Majesty's servant at Dronningborg [see note 2]; Niels Martensen, hospital servant in Aarhus [see note 9]; Frands Pedersen, serving Thames Andersen, Eske Brokkes servant; Rasmus Jensen [or Jonsen], Peder Brahes servant; Jens Jensen, Mogens Jensens servant, hospital servant in Aarhus.

I had them come to me one by one at the church altar and asked everyone especially what and where they had seen the vision on their meadows. The poor men told me individually with so great affection and honesty before God what they had seen that I could not listen to them without feeling pity and crying. Each of them more than once stated by their salvation and eternal wellbeing that they did not tell it at any point different than they have seen it.

I recorded in writing word by word what they individually told me without altering anything. I wish to state before God and all people that their individual statements where much alike. Their shorter and longer accounts were in compliance with each other in a way that made one wonder. If one said more than another, the common details matched with the other stories.

Every knowledgeable person knows that such poor people could not in their fear and horror give attention to all details that happened before their eyes long after [the event]. *It is therefore amazing they all could describe such mysterious and strange experiences, which they could not understand in such detail. Many of the old men, but especially women, confessed that they had not yet overcome the fear they experienced and that it* [the vision] *always appeared before their eyes.*

It also much verified their story that they did not claim to have seen specific details told by others when they were asked about them, but said they did not witness it. They stated by God that they only wanted to state what they have seen.

This is strangely corresponding with good Mr. Hans account that they on their way home after having seen the vision disappear had met some young boys herding some pigs in the fields. They asked them if they had seen anything, which they had not. The boys however said they had heard so heavy a rain shower and storm that it frightened them. It seemed to them that the trees shivered when it came over the forest [see note 10].

After having questioned all about the circumstances in the church I wished that anyone who had the time might come to my farm [probably Rosenholm Castle, approx. 14 km / 9.3 miles away] *the following afternoon and in person tell their stories to my people and servants. Four of the interviewed men came to me soon after I arrived home and in the presence of more than a half hundred persons from my staff and others* retold their stories such as I have recorded it from their own mouths.

I have with honesty and knowledge compiled this to a complete story so that all God fearing people having their natural wits should know and understand what our Heavenly Father had let happen.

[The rest of the account contains lengthy reflections on the work of God and human salvation.]

Holger Rosenkrantz
My hand

I, F. Jonsen, recorded this with my own hand.

NB.
This F. Jonsen was M. Frants Jonsen, who had been Rector Scholae [i.e. principal] *in Slagelse and thereafter in Copenhagen and then parish vicar in Store Heddinge.* [See note 11].

6 List of eyewitnesses

The last pages of Rosenkrantz´s account contain a list of many of those who witnessed the Aarslev event. Some of the listed names are not mentioned in the account.

Neither Rørdam (1886) nor Hansen (1909) included the list in their printed versions of Langebek´s text.

List of names:

The Aarslev villagers listed below have all seen the earlier mentioned omen and state it to be as true as recorded here.

Niels Mikkelsen, nobleman Jørgen Billes servant

Staphen Pedersen, nobleman Eske Borks servant

Peder Tordsen, servant at Dronningborg

Niels Martensen, hospital servant in Aarhus

Rasmus Jensen [or Jonsen], *nobleman Peder Brahes servant*

Mikkel Jensen, servant of Jens Mikkelsen servant at Dronningborg

Jens Jensen and Kirsten Jørgensdatter, both servants of Mogens Jensen hospital servant in Aarhus

Lars Espersen, who is with his father, noble[man?] [unreadable] *Krabbes servant*

34

Frants Pedersen and Margareta Pehrsdatter, both serving Thames Andersen, nobleman Eske Borks servant

Elline Lauritsdatter, serving Mads Jensen, hospital servant in Aarhus

Gertrud Stahphensdatter, aforementioned Staphen Pedersens daughter

Søren Sørensen and Agatha N., both serving Hans Pedersen, parish vicar

And some more

7 Notes

Note 1:
"Servant" is an old expression for someone serving under a king, prince or nobleman. Denmark has during the centuries had different legal systems for owning and leasing land including serfdom, forcing peasants who did not own their farm to serve the landowner and being subject to certain conditions, e.g. to do labour for the landowner. A social reform later abolished the serfdom system.

Peasants were mostly living in villages in 1600. The allocation of farms to the countryside due to agricultural reforms came almost 200 years after the vision on Aarslev Meadows. This may be a reason why Rosenkrantz referred to them as townsmen.

Note 2:
The nearby Dronningborg Manor belonged in 1600 to King Kristian IV of Denmark.

Note 3:
The text uses the Danish term "bøsse", meaning a long-range gun. I have used "musket" as a synonym, even if the term "arquebus" may be more historically correct to describe a low velocity long-range firearm in 1600. A "musket shot" is not a standardised unit of length. An estimated distance of a shot with a late 16th century long-range firearm is about 200 meters / 218 yards. A distance of 3 musket shots may therefore be approx. up to approx. 600 metres / 656 yards. The distance is not exact, but gives an indication of the distance between the peasants and the vision.

Note 4:
Running across 20-30 acres does not indicate that Niels Mikkelsen ran a very long distance. An acre normally consisted of a very small plot of land in 1600.

Note 5:
The district courts (in Danish: Herredsting) were in 1600 even used to spread information of common interest to the community.

Note 6:
"Master" is here used as an academic title. Niels Paaske had a clerical career and became bishop in Bergen, Norway, from 1616 to his death in 1636. Denmark and Norway were in a political and administrative union during the 14th - 19th centuries.

Note 7:
Hansen (1909) points out that the fact that the peasants and the priest met on their way back to the village show that they have been on the meadows southwest of Aarslev.

Note 8:
Eske Brok (or Bork), 1560-1625, was the owner of Gammel Estrup Manor located near Aarslev. Gammel Estrup is now the Danish Manor Museum.

Note 9:
The meaning of the term "hospital servant" in unsure, but seem to mean a person serving a hospital under the church, being a huge landowner in these days.

Note 10:

Hansen (1909) points out that it probably was not Brusgaard Forest, which seem to be too far away, but a thicket whose location is unknown today.

Note 11:

The NB comment is probably Langebek´s own. M[aster] Frants Jonsen is recorded as having been principal at the school attached to Vor Frue Church in Copenhagen 1594 - 1606. He was the first principal to at the same time to function as lector of music at Copenhagen University. He is later recorded as being a parish vicar in Store Heddinge south of Copenhagen in 1610. Frantz Jonson died in 1634.

Frants Jonsen´s relation to Rosenkrantz and his reason for being at Rosenholm Castle during the interviews in 1600 are not known. However, Rosenkrantz mentions in his account that the theologian Niels Paaske accompanied him on his visit to Aarslev Church on May 12th. It seems that Rosenkrantz surrounded himself with theologians / scholars at Rosenholm, probably due to his deep interest in religious matters. Frants Jonsen may have been staying (perhaps employed) at Rosenholm during spring 1600 and given the task of writing down Rosenkrantz´s account.

8 References

Hansen, S. (1909). *Et mærkeligt Syn I Aarslev Enge*. In Aarbog [Yearbook], Randers Amts Historiske Samfund [The Randers Country's Historical Society], pages 79-100. Randers, Denmark, 1909. In Danish.

Langebek, J. (ca. 1760). *Et mærkeligt Syn I Aarslev Enge*. Thottske Samling. No. 1623, 4to. Det Kongelige Bibliotek [The Royal Library], Copenhagen, Denmark. In Danish.

Rørdam, H. F. (1886). *Holger Rosenkrands's Beretning om et underligt Syn i Aaret 1600*. In Kirkehistoriske Samlinger [Church Historic Collection], 1886, coll. 3, V, pages 659-668. Selskabet for Danmarks Kirkehistorie. [The Danish Church Historical Society]. Copenhagen, Denmark. In Danish.